An Essential Guide for the Sugar Free Kitchen!

The Sugar Free
Baking Guide

A must have guide for the sugar free baker!

From the popular
Sugar Free Diva
Website

Includes the popular sugar alternatives to help you decide which ones are best for your baking needs as well as which sugar alternatives should never be used for baking!

You'll love this guide!
Annie Busco

The Sugar Free Alternative Guide

Alternatives to Sugar that can be used in recipes. (with bonus recipes!)

Annie Busco

The Sugar Free Diva

1st Edition

Introduction

It seems as if everyone that I know, who has ever tried to cut back on sugar, has experimented with sugar alternatives in their kitchen creations.

I am no exception. For as long as I can remember, I have been experimenting with alternatives to sugar when baking. Naturally, some results from my experimentation have been more successful than others. However, just like with everything else in life, success is only possible through trial and error.

Thus, I know that my kitchen experiments need to hit a few bumps in the road in order to work out for me in the end.

Baking without adding all of the sugar that normally comes with baked goods is possible. You just have to be open to sweetening without using sugar.

I am not going to go on a rant about sugar and whether or not it is good for you. This book is not about bashing sugar. However, this book is about how to not have to use sugar (or as much sugar) in baking recipes. The reason(s) why you choose to not use sugar is (are) totally up to you.

Also, whether or not you choose to use any of the alternatives in this book is entirely up to you. This book can help you find the alternative to sugar that you can use when you bake.

In my baking experience, there have been six lessons that I have learned which have inspired me to write this book

The Six Lessons that I have Learned from Sugar Free Baking.

Lesson Number 1: When substituting alternatives for sugar in a recipe, there will be some experimentation. This experimentation is a necessary part of the process.

You probably already have experimented with a shampoo or even a certain cereal to see if they would work out for you. The same idea would hold true for baking. In baking sugar free we experiment with our sugar alternatives to make sure that our sweeteners and our methods work out in our recipes.

Using a sugar alternative should offer to a recipe the sweetness and taste just as sugar would add. Obtaining a sweet taste could be our biggest reason for choosing a sugar alternative. But, we also need to be concerned with everything that goes into the mixing bowl and how they interact with one another.

Here is why we would need some experimentation to make sure that our recipe works.
Sugar does more than just sweeten a recipe.

Sugar adds sweetness, volume, and certain other baking properties too. These properties may or may not be replicated when we use an alternative to sugar. The properties really depend upon the alternative that we choose.

Sometimes, the success of a recipe may mean having to make adjustments in the other ingredients that we add to the bowl. As you may expect, the success of a recipe may depend upon the baking methods that we use.

Experimenting helps us work out other issues when we bake with sugar alternatives.

As I have mentioned, when added to a recipe, sugar contributes to the sweet flavor of the food as well as the leavening, browning, and caramelizing that takes place. The shape of sugar also affects results.

When sugar and butter are creamed together in a recipe, it is the shape of the sugar granule that facilitates the creaming process. This is a process that sugar alternatives cannot seem to entirely match. The sugar and butter process yields a perfect cream-like result.

It is for the reasons that I have just mentioned that we should experiment with our sugar alternative recipes to make sure that they work. We need to experiment with the different sugar alternatives, how we use them, and how the alternatives are used in a particular recipe.

Lesson Number 2: Not every sugar alternative is meant to be baked with.

Think of this as being like every person that you have dated in the past who may not have been the kind of person that you would want to marry. Not every suitor was meant to be married to.

I can assure you that I am not the only person who has learned this wrong alternative lesson the hard way. The funny looking cookies or the flat and tasteless bread that resulted when you used a certain sugar alternative may have been a good clue for you as well. I know that it was for me. I now know that value and the importance of experimenting with my recipes.

Not every sugar alternative is meant to be baked. This is because of the chemical makeup of that sugar alternative.

The chemical makeup of some sugar alternatives makes them unsuitable for baking with. The reasoning behind has to do with the temperature that the alternative chemically breaks down at. Some sugar alternatives just cannot take the heat. Oddly enough there are some alternatives that perform well at higher temperatures than others as well.

You will see what I mean by this idea as we move on in the chapters. The point here is to know that you just cannot add any alternative to sugar to your recipe and expect great results when your recipe is in the oven baking. You will also find that certain sugar alternatives work better than most when frozen or brought to high temperatures.

Lesson Number 3: We need to find a good balance in our ingredients in order for a recipe to work for us.

I am talking about looking at the entire mixing bowl. A good way to explain this is to remind you why we like to add salt to foods such as french fries. We like to salt our fries in order to balance out the deep potato flavor, Adding salt seems create the perfect balance of taste that makes fries so easy to eat.

I have already mentioned issues related to the chemical makeup and the need for experimentation when using sugar alternatives. We also have to consider the balance that we strive to create. Balance of taste, which is also part of the experimentation, has to do with everything that is added to the mixing bowl and how they all work together.

In sugar free baking, this balance is about sweetness, volume and moisture.

Sugar has the ability to hold the moisture in our baked goods as well as make them taste sweet and add volume to our creations. When we remove the sugar we need to balance these factors out by other means. Finding the proper balance in our recipes is something that we learn through our experimentations. We can also call this trial and error in baking.

Lesson Number 4: Not everything that we bake using sugar alternatives will taste or look exactly like the sugar containing counterpart.

This should be of little surprise to anyone who is familiar with sugar alternatives. What I mean is that every kind of sweetener has its own taste. You may have noticed this too. Some sugar alternatives taste more like sugar than others do.

Sugar alternatives can also make the baked good look different from its sugar containing counterpart. Here are a couple of great examples for you. When it comes to looking like the baked good which has the sugar, cookies tend to be less flat while bread may not be as big when we use a sugar alternative.

Yeast really loves a bit of sugar to help it rise. The result is a larger loaf of bread when sugar is used versus using certain sugar alternatives. Also, as sugar helps brown baked goods, sugar alternatives do not. The good news is that I will share some hacks that we can use to deal with the browning issues.

Lesson Number 5: Sugar alternatives do not work in every recipe.

A moment ago I mentioned how the shape of sugar leads to the success of creaming butter. Unfortunately, sugar alternatives are not always so successful at this. There are other was in which sugar alternatives cannot fully replicate sugar in a recipe as sugar is able to do.

Because sugar alternatives just do not work in every recipe, there are some recipes that we may have to skip making. We can also find a workaround or hack to make something similar but, not exact. Sometimes, it may mean just try another sugar alternative or using a blend.

Crystallization is another challenge for folks who use sugar alternatives. This is another chemical obstacle that we may find as a challenge besides the obstacle of temperatures and chemical breakdown.

When it comes to sugar alternatives not being able to work in every recipe, this may be one of the best examples. Crystallization from sugar is what makes candy and baked pastries so good. You may remember eating 'rock candy' as a kid. This candy is the best example of sugar crystallization. Sugar alternatives just do not seem to have this ability in their chemical composition.

Lesson Number 6 - Read the labels.

As I will be reminding you throughout this guide, reading the labels on what you add to your recipes is essential. There are many reasons why you should read the label. Among those reasons is that we should always know what we are adding to a recipe before we add it to the recipe.

A label should tell you what is in the product and how to use it.

Look at the ingredient label on the package. You may already do this when you buy other kinds of food such as cereal or a frozen meal. Many sugar alternatives are packaged for use as blended with sugar or even flour to make them usable in recipes.

Sometimes, a label can tell us something that we may not have even thought about. You may find that some sugar alternatives still have calories in them even though they are being sold as a sugar alternative.

A label can also tell you whether or not you should be baking with that product or any side effects that product can have on your body.

These are the six lessons that I have learned.

You may have noticed that many of these lessons may overlap or work together. We will certainly go further into depth of everything that I just mentioned throughout this guide.

Dealing with these lessons should help make you aware that there are some obstacles to baking when you do not add sugar to the mixing bowl. However, you will most likely feel rewarded in the end as well since you had some motivation to go sugar free.

About this Guide.

The purpose of this guide is to help us decide which sugar alternative is best for our baking needs.

As I have mentioned, it is not my intent to tell you to use one alternative over another in a recipe. Perhaps, I may suggest to not use one alternative because it will not yield proper results. Some sugar alternatives are better than others when it comes to baking .

Not every alternative is capable, because of chemical composition, of being baked.

How to use this Guide

I know how I would use this guide. I would read through the entire contents of it first, taking notes especially when there is something that pertains to my needs. I would then go through it again to see if there was anything that I had missed that may also be useful. I would actually do this step periodically as a reminder.

You can use this guide to reference alternatives as well.

For example, when you are looking for a new sugar alternative to try, check out the alternatives listed in this guide. This guide also offers insights on how to use sugar alternatives as well as their equivalence to sugar.

The Sugar Free Diva

This book is a companion guide for the recipes that are shared on TheSugarFreeeDiva.com

You may have stumbled upon a recipe from the SugarFreeDiva website and/or maybe you are a dedicated reader. This guide can be used to help answer questions or clarify ideas when it comes to recipes and the alternatives to use in them. I wrote this guide to answer many of the questions that I have received from my readers.

The purpose of this guide is to explore sugar alternatives in order to find the best one(s) to serve our baking needs.

While you read this book you may learn something new and useful. You will learn that some alternatives work better than others or that your chosen alternative may not be the best one to use for baking. You may even find a new sugar alternative to try out in your recipes.

I have also included some bonus topics.

I have included tidbits, facts, and suggestions for using sugar alternatives. There is a chart which shows alternatives and their equivalency to sugar when used in recipes.

And lastly, I have thrown in a couple of popular recipes from my site.

So, let's get started.

Sweeteners that we use.

Chapter 1
The Available Sweeteners

We like food that tastes sweet right?

Everyone knows that sugar, or an alternative to sugar, needs to be present for a dessert to taste sweet. We also know that there are many faces to sugar, just as there are many faces to the substitutions for sugar. These faces help guide us in making our decisions when it comes to using a sugar alternative.

This book is broken up into sugar and the different options available to use as alternatives to sugar.

<u>Sugar</u>

We will start our investigation with sugar. That way we can compare our alternatives to it.

Since you are reading this I think that you may be like me.

I am a (self-proclaimed) recovering sugar addict. My love affair with sugar started at an early age. Sugar was in a lot of the food that I ate and in a lot of the beverages that I drank. To be honest, when I was a child, there were not a lot of substitutes for sugar available. You either consumed sugar or you did not. People were also less conscious of sugar being in what we consumed back then. Certainly, things have changed over the years.

We know our Sucrose.

Sucrose is a name for sugar that we know best. Yes, there are different kinds of sugar, just as there are different kinds of sugar alternatives available to us.

Sucrose sugar is also referred to as 'table sugar'.

We use sucrose not just to sweeten our food and drinks. Sucrose also adds texture, color, volume, and calories to what we consume. In baked goods, sucrose helps with the browning. Sucrose also feeds the yeast and caramelizes what we create. Sucrose is processed and refined sugar.

Sucrose is not the only sugar out there.

You may have heard of these kinds of sugar too. Fructose, Galactose, Glucose, Lactose and Maltose. Brown sugar is a sugar which contains molasses. In the bonus section of this guide there is a listing of the other names for sugars that you may want to look for.

Knowing the different names of sugars comes in handy when you go to read a nutritional or ingredient label on a package before you make the decision to use or eat what is in it.

The Sugar Alternatives.

We can further divide the sugar alternatives into NATURAL and ARTIFICIAL Sugar Alternatives.

Natural sugar alternatives are derived from natural sources.

At this time we should note that not all natural sugar alternatives are indeed sugar free or even calorie free. They are simply alternatives, to sucrose, that can be used to sweeten something. You may be not even be concerned with these factors.

In this book, we will reference the following natural sugar alternatives;

- Stevia (which is actually regarded as a GRAS and non-nutritive)
- Agave Nectar
- Honey
- Molasses
- Syrup (such as maple syrup)
- Coconut Palm Sugar
- Sugar Alcohols

There are reasons why someone would use a natural sugar alternative in a recipe rather than sugar in the form of sucrose.

We will touch on reasons for using natural sugar alternatives as we proceed.

I do want to point out here that fructose, the sugar found in fruit, is a natural alternative as well. Perhaps, you have used apple sauce or orange juice in the past to sweeten up a recipe.

Many of the natural sugar alternatives are nutritive. That is, they do add calories and carbohydrates to our creations.

Besides being natural or artificial, sugar alternatives are also classified according to how intense they are as a sweetener.

High intensity sweeteners taste hundreds of times as sweet as sugar does to the tongue. Each of these high intensity sweeteners are of different sweetness intensities. However, most of these sweeteners are generally artificial in nature. You are probably familiar with many of these sweeteners by their brand names, which include Splenda and Sweet'N Low.

Artificial Sugar Alternatives

Artificial sugar alternatives, also known as sweeteners, have been created for us.

Artificial sweeteners are non nutritive and non caloric meaning that they do not add calories or nutrition to a recipe. The result is that these sweeteners provide us with low or no calories or carbohydrates. Artificial sweeteners really just add some sweetness to our recipes.

Artificial sugar alternatives are popular because they have little or no impact on blood sugar.

When an artificial sweetening product adds nothing other than taste to a recipe, there is no sugar added to the blood stream from using that sweetener.

If that artificial sweetener is a high intensity sweetener, it can be hundreds of times sweeter to the tongue than sugar is. As a result, we may need to use less of that high intensity sugar alternative than we would use sugar in a recipe.

This is why we need to know how much of the high intensity sweetener to add when we replace the sugar with it in order to make something remain sweet to the taste.

Needing less of these alternatives in a recipe may mean bulking up the sugar alternative product with other ingredients to make it equal to sugar in volume.

We touched on this in the last chapter when we discussed the need to read product labels as well as experiment with our recipes.

Sometimes a sugar alternative is packaged to make substitution easier for us to use by making it equal to sugar in volume.

Many artificial sugar alternatives are sold already bulked up in order to make it a volume equivalent, which is why it is important to read the label of the container before using it. It may be bulked up with sugar or even flour.

Sugar Free Butter Cream Icing
TheSugarFreeDiva.com

Sugar alternatives from nature.

Chapter 2
Natural Alternatives to Sugar

Technically, sugar is natural - right? So why would we use a natural alternative to sugar in recipes? There are actually some good reasons for this, as you may learn.

We touched on the natural alternatives briefly in the last chapter. Now we will discuss them further.

Stevia

Stevia seems to be the sugar alternative darling these days for many of us.

I think that much of this popularity may be because Stevia is that one sweetener that is considered to be both natural and high intensity. Many people may be wary about putting chemicals from artificial sweeteners into their body. Stevia is a natural way to add sweetness without all of those chemicals. It is kind of like having the best of both worlds.

There is not a lot of research on Stevia in the United States (USA) at this point.

For this reason the Food and Drug Administration (FDA) has not fully recognized stevia as a food additive. However, the FDA does allow for the use of stevia as a GRAS. This is a confusing thought for the average person. So, to make a long story short, some products with stevia in them, in the USA are 'lawful' for use.

There are some folks who argue that stevia can even be healthy to eat. I am not an expert on this and I am only trying to relay the information, as I know it, to you.

What Stevia is.

Stevia is natural and is derived from the stevia rebaudiana Bertoni plant from South America. The stevia sweetener that we use is a non nutritive sweetener (no calories, no carbs), unless it has been combined in packaging with something else, which is often done.

In its pure form, stevia is 200-400 times sweeter that sugar - making it a high intensity sweetener. I have mentioned that stevia is a natural and non nutritive sugar alternative.

Stevia is sold as a liquid, powder, or pure extract.

Also, in the USA, stevia is often combined or blended with fillers such as sugar. Bulking stevia up is often done to make it a 1:1 alternative to sugar in a recipe. When it is bulked up it is sometimes called a 'blend'. Being 1:1 means that for every cup of sugar that we may add to a recipe, for example, we can use 1 cup of of the alternative instead. It is really a volume of ingredients idea more than anything.

How to Use Stevia.

Because of stevia's chemical composition, we usually will adjust baking by lowering the baking temperature and baking longer in order to promote browning. Stevia bakes faster than sugar which is why we adjust the baking of it.

Stevia is often a bit more expensive to purchase than most sugar alternatives are. However, we hear fewer complaints about the side effects from eating stevia than we do with other alternatives.

Agave Nectar

I must say that I am intrigued with a sweetener that comes from the same plant as tequila comes from. That certainly sounds like someone(s) is maximizing the uses for the Agave plant.

The truth is that, according to the experts, pure agave nectar, or agave as some folks refer to it as, has more calories than table sugar does (60 versus 40 per tablespoon). Agave is high in fructose yet, it digests slower that sugar digests in the body. A slower digestion can mean a slower sugar flow through the blood.

We use agave nectar in beverages, marinades and some baked items.

How to use Agave in recipes.

It is recommended that you reduce the liquid in a recipe to counterbalance the liquid that is added by adding the agave. Also, combine the agave with the other liquids from the ingredient listing before adding it to the recipe. Reduce the oven temperature about 20 degrees when baking for best results.

Honey

I love that honey is made by bees.

What could be more natural than that? You may have read studies that suggest that honey is more than just a sweetener. We all seem to know people who like to eat honey for its 'health' benefits. They believe that honey can be used for allergies and for the healing of cuts and sore throats. I do not know if all of this is true but, I certainly do like the thought of all of the possibilities for honey.

Honey does have carbohydrates and sugar in it.

It also has B Vitamins, antioxidants, potassium and minerals, according to the experts. When compared to table sugar, honey scores close to sugar in calories and glycemic index.

Honey is 25-50% sweeter than sugar.

Adding honey to baked goods can make the results more moist and dense as well. However, honey tends to brown baked foods faster.

How to bake with honey.

Because honey browns food faster, I like to reduce the oven temperature by 20-25 degrees when I bake with it. Also, when using more than one cup of honey in a recipe, we need to offset the other liquids by a quarter cup and add 1/2 teaspoon of baking soda. I hear that when added to coffee cakes, honey makes the world a great place to live in.

Molasses

I must say that when it comes to recipe substitutions, molasses is one of the hard choices to figure out.

Sometimes, I can get away with using a sugar free syrup as a substitute for the taste that molasses gives to a recipe. But, using syrup really does not lend to the exact same taste as if I had used molasses. Molasses is famous for its rich taste and brown color. It is pretty hard to make a perfect gingerbread anything or decent baked bean dish without molasses in it.

Molasses is the byproduct of sugar cane becoming sugar.

Molasses is not as sweet to the tongue as sugar and it is not used as much as an alternative to sugar as a result. This is partly because we would need to add more molasses than we would have to add sugar in a recipe to make that recipe taste as sweet.

Did I mention that molasses has 950 calories in one cup while white sugar has 740?

Black strap molasses is a popular variety of molasses.

Black strap molasses is said to be more mineral and vitamin rich. Folks who are concerned about their blood sugar like that this variety of molasses is digested more slowly that regular sugar.

I would caution anyone from consuming molasses straight out of the bottle as this is a taste that is hard to get rid of in the mouth.

How to use molasses in a recipe.

I think that I can sum this up in two words. Go Easy. Molasses is rich, thick, and sweet. I usually use molasses sparingly and just in those holiday cookies that require it or I may use it in something like baked beans. There are a lot of calories in molasses which can also sway your decision of whether or not to use it.

Syrup

When I think of syrup, I think of the natural syrup that comes from maple trees.

In my mind, those maple trees are located in some amazingly beautiful area of the country where the air is clean and the people are as nice as the scenery.

As a bit of a disclosure, I do own a restaurant where syrup is a big deal. Serving the right syrup can certainly make or break a meal - at least as far as my patrons are concerned.

I hate that I have yet to hear of a natural maple syrup that is also sugar free.

On the rare occasion that I do use sugar free syrup in a recipe that I share it is because I am trying to offer a sugar free alternative to folks who just cannot have the regular maple syrup. I also like to substitute sugar free syrup for molasses in certain recipes such as sugar free holiday cookie baking.

The reality is that maple syrup is more sweet than sugar is.

One tablespoon of maple syrup, in its natural form, has about 55 calories whereas sugar has about 48 calories. Both have similar glycemic effects.

How to use Maple Syrup in Recipes.

Maple syrup is an especially good sugar alternative to use in candy making. It is used primarily for its taste. Maple fudge would be a good example for this.

When used in regular baking recipes, use 3/4 maple syrup to one white sugar (such as 3/4 cup for every one cup of sugar). For every cup of maple syrup that is added, reduce your other liquids by 3 tablespoons to compensate.

Sugar free syrup on the other hand, I have used in conjunction with a granular sugar alternative to get a sugar free result that may mimic a molasses or regular syrup recipe.

Corn Syrup

While we are on the subject of using syrups as sugar alternatives, I should mention corn syrup. Corn syrup is popular for use in candy - as in hard candy - because it does not crystalize (get hard). Corn syrup does have calories and carbohydrates but, it is fat free.

How to use corn syrup in recipes.

As mentioned, corn syrup does have calories and carbohydrates in it. Because it is liquid, it is not suitable in most baked recipes. Corn syrup works best in candy making that is, candy that is not sugar free.

Coconut Palm Sugar

Coconut palm sugar gained attention a few years ago when a famous 'TV doctor' raved about it on his talk show.

The TV doctor was selling us on the idea that coconut palm sugar is a great alternative to brown sugar when used in our recipes.

Here is what coconut palm sugar believers say.

There is a theory shared by this TV doctor, that because coconut palm sugar is thought to have a low glycemic index, it is the ideal choice to make when choosing a sugar alternative. It would be safer on the sugar in blood and thus, preferred for anyone watching the sugar in their blood.

Since coconut palm sugar is dark in nature, it seems as if it would work well in many recipes that call for brown sugar.

Coconut palm sugar would be a 1:1 alternative to brown sugar in baked goodies only with a lower glycemic index, according to the theory shared by the TV talk show doctor.

Yes, after I first heard that famous doctor promote coconut palm sugar, I used it in my chocolate chip cookies. I think that in my mind, because this famous TV doctor endorsed coconut palm sugar as a sugar alternative, then it must be lower in sugar and thus, good for me to use too.

Here is something else.

Since all of that TV doctor 'hoopla'(for lack of a better term) came out, there have been some other folks who have come out and have shared theories that may seem to be to the contrary of what the doctor said.

The moral of the story I suppose is that you should probably research this alternative, just like any other. Make sure that coconut palm sugar is for you before you use it.

What I can tell you is that coconut palm sugar is derived from nectar from the coconut palm tree.

According to the American Diabetes Association, at the time of this writing, coconut palm sugar can be used as a sweetener. Many experts seem to agree that it can be used in moderation - kind of like table sugar.

How to use Coconut Palm Sugar in recipes.

Coconut palm sugar is a lot like white sugar in some ways. Coconut palm sugar and white sugar have the same calorie and carbohydrate count. However, the burning point of coconut palm sugar is at a lower point than regular sugar.

This means that coconut palm sugar breaks down at a lower oven temperature than sugar. This is something to keep in mind when using coconut palm sugar on the stove or even baking with it. I would either lower the baking temperature or bake for less time or both.

The granules of coconut palm sugar are composed a bit differently than regular or brown sugar. As a result, it is not as successful when used to cut butter. Coconut palm sugar is also not as good as regular white sugar when it comes to holding moisture.

When using coconut palm sugar while baking I will sometimes add a bit extra fat and liquid to a recipe to help maintain that moisture balance.

Also, when purchasing coconut palm sugar it is important to read the label on the package.

The package will mention if it is 100% organic coconut palm sugar with no fillers. If you do not see this on the label, that specific coconut palm sugar may not be the best choice for your needs.

Sugar Alcohols

The last natural sugar alternative that I want to mention would be sugar alcohols.

If you have ever felt the ill effects from eating too much candy that is labeled 'sugar free' then you may have felt the effects of sugar alcohol.

It is not an uncommon thing for someone trying sugar free candy for the first time to eat more of that candy than they should eat. The result can be an intestinal upset issue from the sugar alcohols used to sweeten the candy.

The moral of the story is that just because the candy is labeled as being 'sugar free' it may not be a good idea to eat a lot of it at one time.

Sugar alcohols are the sugar alternative that we see most often in sugar free candy and gum.

We rarely use sugar alcohols for cooking and baking.

Examples of sugar alcohols that you may have seen in the past may include;

- Xylitol

- Sorbitol

- Erythritol

- Mannitol

- Maltitol

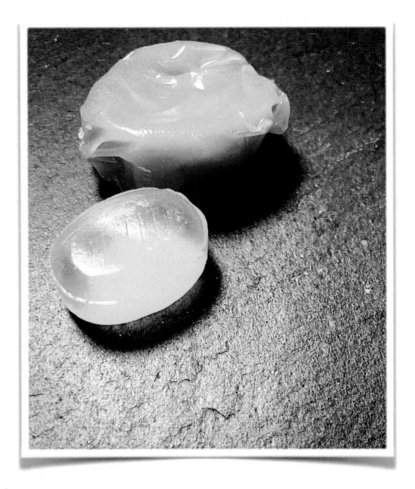

Candy manufacturers seem to like sugar alcohols because they are relatively cheap to use. We also may like that sugar alcohols have little affect on the sugar in the blood.

However, we should enjoy sugar alcohols in moderation as they can be a problem for our gastrointestinal system.

How to use sugar alcohols in recipes.

I would use sugar alcohols in candy making and stick to the recipe.

Read the ingredient label on the sugar free candy that you purchase as well.

As mentioned, consuming sugar alcohols should be done in moderation due to the gastrointestinal side effects that are possible from consumption.

The non-natural alternatives to sugar.

Chapter 3
The Artificial Alternatives to Sugar

Artificial sugar alternatives are probably the most commonly used sugar alternatives that we see used in prepared products. I use them quite often when I am in the kitchen. What I like about the artificial sweeteners that I use is that they generally have low to no carbohydrates and calories in them.

Artificial sweeteners are non nutritive and non caloric when not packaged with fillers or other items.

These sugar alternatives are high intensity sweeteners which means that they are hundreds of times sweeter than sugar. Being high intensity means that you would need to use less of these artificial sweeteners in a recipe that you would use sugar, if it were in that same recipe. Doing so would be to yield the same level sweetness to the tongue in that recipe as if you had used sucrose.

Artificial sweeteners are another important product to read the label on before using.

Most notably, how much to use in a recipe. If your product label tells you to use your high intensity alternative in a 1:1 ratio as you would use sugar in a recipe, then your high intensity sweetener may have had something added to it to 'bulk' it up. Think about when you used something labeled 'condensed' and the instructions said to use less of the product than you would normally use. The regular product that your condensed product is replacing may have had water added to it to 'bulk' it up.

It should make sense that we use less of the high intensity sweetener to get to the same level of sweetness as sugar just like with that condensed product that we just discussed.

Read the label on the package to see the ingredients and the equivalence to sugar before you use it - my recommendation to you. Often, these sweeteners will be blended with sugar with a result of being 'lower sugar' rather than 'sugar free'.

The artificial sweeteners that I will mention are;

- Sucralose

- Aspartame

- Saccharin

Sucralose

In the USA, the FDA has approved Sucralose as high intensity sweetener food additive.

That means that the FDA thinks it is okay to use Sucralose in our food as an additive and that Sucralose is also pretty sweet in taste to the tongue.

Sucralose is a high intensity sweetener.

As a high intensity sweetener, Sucralose is sweeter than sugar. Sucralose is 600 times sweeter than regular white table sugar (sucrose). For this reason, many of the containers of Sucralose that are available for purchase from the store may have been 'bulked' up in order to make it a 1:1 alternative to sugar.

Bulking up the Sucralose product sold in the store makes it easier for us to substitute it in to recipes as a 1:1 alternative equivalent to sugar.

However, Sucralose also has calories.

One cup of Sucralose has about 50 calories in it. Which, in the scheme of things in a recipe, may not amount to a lot of calories in a recipe serving. There are also about 12 carbohydrates in that cup of Sucralose.

Sucralose can be good choice for an alternative when baking.

This is because it is heat stable and will hold on to its sweet taste. Splenda is a popular brand of Sucralose.

How to use Sucralose in a recipe.

As mentioned, read the product label to learn how much of that Sucralose product is equivalent to a specific amount of sugar, such as a cup, in a recipe.

Try to stick to a granular Sucralose product when substituting it for a granular sugar. Keep an eye on the oven while baking as baked products with Sucralose in them may bake faster.

Finally, adjust the recipe in the future as needed for baking times, oven temperatures and the moisture in the product.

Aspartame

Aspartame has been approved in the USA as a "nutritive sweetener" as it does have calories.

The FDA categorizes it as a food additive. It is about 200 times sweeter than sugar as it is also considered to be a high intensity sweetener. Because aspartame is low in calories (about four calories per gram), some folks categorize it as a nonnutritive sweetener like most high intensity sweeteners.

Aspartame tends to break down easily when heated, making it not the best candidate for baking.

Instead of adding aspartame to our baked creations, we tend to see it in beverages or in packets on a table in a restaurant to be used in coffee etc.

Popular aspartame products that we often see include Nutrasweet or Equal.

Folks with PKU (Phenylketonuria) are advised to stay away from this sweetener.

How to use Aspartame in a recipe.

Stick to non-baked recipes or other sugar alternatives instead.

Saccharin

There was a time when saccharin was the only option available for when looking for an alternative to sugar.

I think that I referenced this earlier when discussing my upbringing with sugar. About 40 years ago, there were some studies done linking saccharin to cancer in rodents and then later on there were more studies done negating those original studies.

Saccharin is an FDA approved nonnutritive sweetener.

Being approved means that the FDA says it is okay to use saccharin. As a nonnutritive sweetener, saccharin adds no calories or nutritional value to whatever we add it to. Saccharin is considered to be a high-intensity sweetener 200 - 700 times sweeter than sugar.

We see saccharin in beverages, in packets on restaurant tables, and even in some recipes.

Saccharin is relatively stable when baked which means that it can be used in lieu of sugar for sweetness in recipes.

However, saccharin differs from sugar in its volume, moisture and ability to brown in recipes. This is not unlike other sugar alternatives that are mentioned in this chapter

How to use Saccharin in recipes.

To maintain a better volume in your baked goods when using saccharin you could blend it with sugar before adding it to the recipe. This may also help maintain moisture in your baked goods and aid in the browning of what you are baking. I'll discuss this a bit more later on.

Adding sweetness without adding sugar.

Chapter 4
Using Sugar Alternatives in Baking

Giving up sugar doesn't have to mean giving up our favorite baked goods, such as cookies and cakes.

Baking with a sugar alternative can certainly save us a few calories. It can also allow people with a sugar sensitivity the ability to enjoy sweet foods from the oven.

As I have mentioned throughout this book, sugar substitutes react differently to heat and to baking than regular white table sugar does. Many of the sugar alternatives that I use heat faster than sugar does. As a result, I need to alter my recipes to accommodate the difference. One way to alter my recipes is to knock a few minutes off of the baking time and set the oven for a lower temperature. I have learned to do this through my experimentation.

Another common problem with sugar alternatives has to do with moisture.

Many sugar alternatives tend to not hold as much moisture as sugar does. As a result, sugar free baked goods may turn out less moist and more dry to the taste. Texture will be affected as well. You may have noticed that because of this moisture issue, many baked foods that are sugar free may not have the shelf life of their sugared counterparts.

Possibly the biggest tip that I can share with you concerning baking sugar free is this.

Always read the package of what ever you are buying to use as a sugar alternatives.

Reading the label is important because not reading it can have implications, including a recipe fail. Here is what I look for on a label before I bring home a potential sugar alternative for use in a recipe;

- Read the contents of the package. Especially to learn whether the packaged contents have been bulked up with other ingredients.

- Can this product be used in baked recipes? Not all sugar alternatives work well when heated thanks to their chemical structure.

- What are the side effects of this sugar alternative? Also, consuming how much of the product may cause a problem (such as when consuming large amounts of sugar alcohols).

- What is the equivalence of this product to sugar in a recipe? Many of the common sugar alternatives are packaged in a 1:1 equivalence which means if a recipe calls for one cup of sugar than one cup of this product is suitable for use. However, most high intensity sweeteners are not 1:1 in equivalency.

- Also, look for any product warnings that may be a problem for you.

When using sugar alternatives in lieu of sugar, there may be some other adjustments that may be needed besides adjusting your baking strategy.

As mentioned, many of the sugar alternatives that we use can dry out a recipe. Adding additional liquids or fat can alleviate this issue.

Also, using a high intensity sweetener may mean that you need less of that sweetener than you would need of sugar.

Adjusting a recipe usually takes some trial and error.

Your adjusted recipe may not work the first time that you make it. Maybe it turned out too dry or not sweet enough for you. Sometimes I find that I should have used a different sugar alternative or maybe gone with brown sugar in addition to my alternative for white sugar and settled for a low sugar result rather than a sugar free result.

The point is that you may need to adjust your recipe and try it again. This is not an uncommon thing for anyone who has been in a kitchen before.

Here are some more tips that you may find useful in your sugar free baking.

Sugar free alternatives can lead to a smaller volume in batter if you are baking a cake or brownies.

You can compensate for this by using a smaller pan. For example, a 6" square and rather than an 8" one for baking brownies or a cake.

Sugar alternatives can turn the resulted baked good lighter in color than if sugar had been used.

This is because the alternatives do not have the ability to brown or caramelize like sugar does.

Sugar has the ability to hold on to moisture. Alternatives do not.
Moisture can affect the texture and density of our baked goods. Texture and density are especially important to breads and cakes.

Here are some sugar free baking hacks for you.

- **Sugar alternatives generally bake faster than normal baked goods.** We need to make adjustments, as discussed, for best results.

- **When baking bread, browning may be a problem for sugar alternatives.** You can lower the heat and bake the item for a few minutes longer or try spraying it lightly with vegetable spray before placing it into the oven for baking.

- **When baking with a saccharine-based sugar alternative,** you will probably have better results using a product that is sweetened with both saccharine and sugar in it. However, it will be low sugar rather than sugar free.

- **Sugar free alternatives affect the texture of baked goods**. The texture of whatever you are baking may not be as moist as desired. Adding a bit of mashed avocado is one way to combat this texture issue.

- **Adding some honey to your recipe can also battle that dry and dense structure.** When baking with honey, it is a good idea to reduce the oven temperature by as much as 25 degrees.

- **Since honey is considered to be a liquid in a recipe,** as opposed to a dry ingredient, some additional adjustments to the other added liquids may be needed as well.

- **Granular sugar alternatives work best in certain recipes.** I usually will state in a recipe that a granular alternative will work best. One instance of this will be when we need to cream the sugar alternative with butter (most of my cookie recipes call for this). Because of the structure of the granular alternative granule itself, air pockets are able to form in the creaming process. These pockets make the creaming of the sugar alternative and butter more successful.

- **Of all the sugar alternatives that are not natural**, aspartame is the one that is most not recommended for baking with.

- **I know that I have mentioned this more than once, but it is important.** Always read the packaging of what you are adding to your recipes before you use it in your recipes - for best results.

- **Adding extracts, such as vanilla extract,** can help balance out the change in taste of something. This is the change in taste that occurs when you remove the sugar from the recipe. I usually increase my extract that I add to recipes that call for it.

- **The volume of a baked good can take a hit** when we remove the sugar from it. Substituting two egg whites for a whole egg is one way to counteract this.

- **One way to fight the volume issue in bread is to add some nonfat dry milk to the recipe.** For every half cup of sweetener in bread add 1/4 cup of nonfat dry milk and 1/4 teaspoon of baking soda. Sometimes I may just add an extra package of yeast and a tablespoon of table sugar.

- **Oddly enough, on the flip side, cookies that are made with sugar alternatives** may have problems becoming flat. Sometimes I like the round golf ball shaped cookies. Other times I will simply flatten the dough with my hand or a fork prior to placing it in the oven for baking to yield a more normal looking cookie.

- **If you are a real fan of certain chewy or crunchy cookies,** such as the classic chocolate chip cookie, that normally calls for brown sugar, you could try using coconut palm sugar instead. Another option would be to consider keeping the brown sugar in the recipe and making a low sugar cookie (just substituting an alternative for the white sugar). This would yield a 'low sugar' rather than a 'sugar free' cookie. Substituting just the white sugar with an alternative will help maintain that chewy or crunchy cookie that you may like better than worrying about being completely sugar free.

- **We know that using sugar alternatives rather than sugar in a cookie recipe can result in a dryer cookie.** We also know that some cookies are meant to be dry even before we make them dryer by using a sugar alternative. One method of dealing with this super dry cooking is to just make it a smaller cookie. Making a smaller cookie than its sugar containing cookie counterpart could make the cookie easier to eat.

- **Yeast works better when sugar feeds it.** You can keep a bit of sugar in your bread recipe for the yeast. What I do with bread, for example, is activate the yeast with warm water and sugar before I start the dough process. A tablespoon of sugar should not have a huge effect on the sugar content of a single slice of bread.

- **Since oven temperatures and baking times need to be adjusted when using sugar alternatives,** it is a good idea to keep an eye on your baked goods while they bake. Start doing this about five to ten minutes prior to the end of the actual recommended baking time.

- **Lastly, sugar alcohols do work better than other alternatives in certain circumstances.** This is because sugar alcohols are more tolerant of higher and lower temperatures. Thus, sugar alcohols work well in candy and ice cream. Just be sure to eat these products in moderation of course, because of possible side effects.

How much should you use?

Chapter 5
Equivalents Used in Baking

As you may have noticed in the past four chapters, the amount of sugar alternative that may be used in a recipe may not be in 1:1 equivalence to sugar itself.

If a recipe calls for 1 cup of sugar, and you would rather use an alternative instead, you may not need 1 cup of that alternative to achieve the same level of sweetness.

One way to find out how much alternative to use is to read the package that the sugar alternative came in. That package should tell you how much of that product is equivalent to, for example, 1 cup of sugar. I know that I have mentioned this before but, it is a good idea to follow for the success of your baking.

There are other reasons why you may want to adjust your equivalents as well.

One reason may be that you are using a high intensity sweetener. You probably remember me mentioning this. High intensity sweeteners can be as much as hundreds of times sweeter than regular sugar. That could have some sweet - as in too sweet - results for what you are baking.

So here are my suggested measurement adjustments that you can use when you bake with sugar alternatives.

Keep in mind that different brand names will have sweeteners in different packaging forms that may differ in equivalents.

Here are equivalents to Measure Sugar Alternatives

1 cup of sugar=

Agave Nectar*- 2/3 cup

Coconut Palm Sugar- 1 cup

Erythritol- 1 1/3 cup

Equal - 25 packets or EQUAL SPOONFUL 1 cup

Honey - substitute 1/2 to 2/3 cup honey.

Maple Syrup- 1/2 cup

Molasses - 1/2 cup

SPLENDA® NO CALORIE SWEETENER, GRANULATED- 1 cup

SPLENDA® No Calorie Sweetener and SPLENDA® Naturals Stevia Sweetener Packets - 24 packets

Also, **SPLENDA® Sugar Blend** - 1/2 cup

SPLENDA® Brown Sugar Blend - 1 cup

Stevia - Equivalent Stevia powdered extract 1 teaspoon or Equivalent Stevia liquid concentrate 1 teaspoon

SweetLeaf®- 24 packets or 2 tbsp shaker or 4 tsp drops or 1/2 tsp extract powder or 2/3 cup Sugarloaf

Truvia Natural Sweetener - 1/3 cup+ 1 1/2 tbs or 24 packets.

Truvia Brown Sugar Blend- 1/2 cup

Also, Truvia Baking Blend- 1/2 cup

Truvia Nectar- 1/4 cup+ 1 tbsp+ 2 tsp

Xylitol- 1 cup

Honey - For every cup used subtract 1/4 cup of other liquids from the recipe, add 1/4 teaspoon baking soda and reduce the temperature of the oven by 25°F rather than the usual temperature as well.

Agave - Reduce the liquid in the recipe by 1/4 cup rather than the full amount--Also, this substitution will also work for Demerara Sugar, Turbinado Sugar, Evaporated Cane Juice, or Sucanat as well

A bit of FYI..

Chapter 6
Extra Information Just For You

Facts, Fictions and Tidbits about Sugar Alternatives

I am not endorsing or trying to sway anyone with the information in the book. The information in this book is intended to be for reference and may or may not be science - at least on my behalf.

When it comes to using sugar alternatives there is a lot of information that we can all use and learn from. A lot of it can amaze you or assist you in your choices. I urge you to read up on what you may want to learn more about with some of the links that I have provide below.

Here are some sugar alternative tidbits for you.

Many of these you have read already in this book or may know of on your own,

1.   **There are categories of sugar alternatives that you may be familiar with.** These categories are natural and artificial sweeteners.

2.   **Natural sweeteners, such as stevia**, are derived from natural sources such as plants.

3.   **Artificial sweeteners,** such as saccharin and aspartame, are created via a **chemical process.**

4.   **Sugar alcohols, such as sorbitol and mannitol,** come from plant products such as fruits. These usually come already added to products rather than us purchasing them to add to our creations.

5.   **You may have wondered if sugar alternatives sold in the United States are safe.** According to the American Diabetes Association, and the National Cancer Institute, yes. They say that there is no significant evidence that any of the sugar substitutes approved for use in the United States cause cancer or other serious health problems.

6.   **Have you ever baked with 'natural sweeteners'?** We know them as 'natural sweeteners'. However, they can have sugar in them and thus, affect us and our blood as sugar would. Natural sweeteners that are used include honey, maple syrup, Agave Nectar, and Molasses.

Read about the research

1.   **The NIH (National Institute of Health) says that a sugar substitutes are a food additive that duplicates the effect of sugar in taste.**

These sugar alternatives usually have less food energy than sugar. This means that consuming a sugar alternative probably will not give you the energy that you may get from a regular candy bar.

2.   **Besides categorizing sweeteners by natural and artificial, sweeteners are also categorized by intensity.**

High intensity sweeteners are hundreds of times sweeter than sugar. High intensity sweeteners would include artificial sweeteners and stevia sweetener.

3.   **You should probably read the labels before you purchase sweeteners.**

This is because some sugar substitutes are "blends" or "mixes". You can add a blend or mix to your recipe. However, you may be adding some sugar too because they contain a mix of the sugar substitute and actual sugar.

4.   Some folks add sugar in the form of 'blends' when baking.

This is because the sugar is important for moisture, browning, and rising. Sugar and yeast have a relationship when brought together in a recipe. Other blends may include flour and are helpful when baking (another reason to read the label).

You may want to know what is sugar free anyway

According to Medline, a sugar free food has less than ½ gram of sugar per serving.

This means that there can be sugar in something that you think is sugar free. Remember that your portions can add up so reading the label can be important to you.

Another FYI from the same source, a calorie-free food has fewer than 5 calories per serving and a reduced-calorie food has at least one-quarter fewer calories than the original food.

Also...

1.   Using artificial sweeteners in place of sugar can help prevent dental decay.

As you know, this is according to the experts. This is one big reason why I try to avoid sugar.

2.   The FDA says that aspartame is safe for the general population under certain conditions.

However, people with a rare hereditary disease known as PKU have a difficulty with this sweetener . If you have PKU you should probably use something else.

3.   High-intensity sweeteners include Saccharin and Aspartame.

These are many times sweeter than sugar. However, they are calorie free or low in calories.

4.   You may be consuming more calories in something prepackaged and purchased from the store even though it is sugar free.

It is common for manufacturers to mask the lack of a sweet taste or issues with texture in something by adding something additional such as fats.

5.   Stevia may help you lower your blood pressure.

There is some research which suggests that Stevia might lower blood sugar levels. Also, if you have diabetes and you eat stevia you should monitor your blood sugar.

6.   Also, consuming Stevia might have act like a water pill or "diuretic." This too is according to the research.

7.   The amount of artificial sweeteners that you consume in the United States are regulated by the FDA

The FDA has set an acceptable daily intake which is the amount that you can consume.

The next section is about certain alternatives that see often.

1.   **Aspartame** - such as Equal, is 220 times sweeter than sucrose (sugar). You cannot bake with it, as many of us have probably tried (raising my hand). This is because it loses its sweetness when exposed to heat. Thus, aspartame is seen a lot in beverages that we enjoy instead of food.

2.   **Splenda** is 600 times sweeter than sugar.
One reason why this is so popular is because we can use it in so many ways. We can bake with it. And we can add it to beverages. Also, we can simply serve it with coffee and tea.

3.   **Saccharin** - Do you remember Sweet'N Low? This is 200 to 700 times sweeter than sucrose (sugar). Saccharin has been around for over 100 years. Many folks say that that there is a specific aftertaste that comes from drinking something with saccharin in it.

4.   **Stevia is a popular sweetener with my readers.** The popularity of Stevia may have something to do with it being a plant-based sweetener. The Stevia that we buy can be up to 300 times sweeter than sugar. This is why a recipe is adjusted as we need less Stevia than we would need sugar to sweeten it

5.   **The lesser known (in the USA) Neotame** is used in diet foods and beverages. From what I have read, this is an artificial sweetener made by the folks at NutraSweet. It is between 7,000 and 13,000 times sweeter than sucrose (sugar).

6.   **Monk Fruit sugar alternative is a powdered extract from monk fruit**. Monk fruit is a melon found in Asia. This sweetener can be up to 200 times sweeter than sucrose (sugar). It is sweeter than sugar and thus, a recipe must be adjusted to use this.

You can find a lot of research out there on about every kind of sugar alternative. The research can help you make decisions on the best sugar alternatives for your needs. I bake a lot but, I also like to vary my choices. I use certain sweeteners specifically for certain recipes as they seem to work better.

The Other Names for Sugar.

By now you may be thinking that I like to remind you to read the labels on products. Here is one more reason to read those labels - to look for sugar under a different name.

This listing was featured on myplate.gov.

The many names for sugar.

If you are avoiding eating sugar, you may want to get familiar with these names for sugars.

- Anhydrous Dextrose

- Confectioners or Powdered Sugar

- Dextrose

- Fructose

- Granulated Sugar

- Syrup

- Sucrose

- Nectar

- Maltose

- Brown Sugar

- Corn Syrup

- High Fructose Corn Syrup

- Honey

- Malt Syrup

- Molasses

- Raw Sugar

- White Sugar

- Invert Sugar

Where You Can Learn More

Start your research with these recommended sites.

Mayo Clinic -> http://www.mayoclinic.org/healthy-living/nutrition-and-healthy-eating/in-depth/artificial-sweeteners/art-20046936?pg=1 ->Artificial Sweeteners and Other Sugar Substitutes.

From MedilinePlus https://medlineplus.gov/ency/article/007492.htm

->Sweeteners - sugar substitutes

https://medlineplus.gov/druginfo/natural/682.html->Information on Stevia

U.S. Food and Drug Administration href="http://www.fda.gov/Food/IngredientsPackaging%20Labeling/FoodAdditives%20Ingredients/ucm397716.htm ->High-Intensity Sweeteners

Read about Saccharin https://www.fda.gov/Food/IngredientsPackagingLabeling/FoodAdditivesIngredients/ucm397725.htm#Saccharin

Learn about Aspartame https://www.fda.gov/Food/IngredientsPackagingLabeling/FoodAdditivesIngredients/ucm397725.htm#Aspartame

Read about Sucralose https://www.fda.gov/Food/IngredientsPackagingLabeling/FoodAdditivesIngredients/ucm397725.htm#Sucralose"

Find out about Steviol glycosides https://www.fda.gov/Food/IngredientsPackagingLabeling/FoodAdditivesIngredients/ucm397725.htm#Steviol_glycosides

https://thesugarfreediva.com/how-to-measure-sugar-alternatives/

https://thesugarfreediva.com/use-high-intensity-sweeteners/

Bonus Section
Chapter 7
Recipes

I thought that I would throw in a couple of my post popular recipes as a bonus.
While these recipes have been on the SugarFreeDiva for a bit of time, they have proven to be popular. They will also be featured in an upcoming book that I am currently working on.

How to make Sugar Free **Powdered Sugar**

TheSugarFreeDiva.com

How to Make Sugar Free Powdered Sugar

Sugar free powdered sugar is something that I use quite often in other recipes. There are several ways to make it-depending on the sweetener that you use.

Any time there is a sugar free cheat for something I get excited.

As bakers, we use powdered, also known as confectioners, sugar quite often. We can make icing out this or add it to another recipe.

There is a downside for us when we use powdered sugar in our recipes.

The downside it that powdered sugar a sugar. This is a sugar that is seriously sweet. Luckily, we can make our own powdered sugar alternative that is also sugar free. We make our own powdered or confectioners sugar that is also sugar free.

How to Make Sugar Free Powdered Sugar

Making your own sugar free powdered sugar is relatively easy to do

The basic recipe for powdered sugar.

Sift or blend together 3/4 cups of a granular Sucralose sweetener such as Splenda and 2 tablespoons cornstarch. Use this recipe as you would use powdered sugar.

Alternative recipe to use:

Use a food processor or blender to combine together the following:

• Sugar free (read the label) nonfat dry milk powder - 2 cups

• Cornstarch-- 2 cups

• Granular Sucralose sweetener such as Splenda--1 cup

Blend the above together until you achieve that powdered sugar consistency.

Stevia recipe

When using Stevia products, such as Truvía®, choose a baking blend in this recipe. You can combine 1 teaspoon of corn starch per 1 cup of this Stevia contained baking blend. Once you have combined these ingredients, you can use a blender or food processor to blend (on high).

No Sugar Added Oatmeal and Raisin Cookies

What you will need to make this recipe.

- Sugar Alternative (granular works best) - Equivalent to 1 1/2 cups of sugar.

- Butter - 2 sticks softened (can sub in 1/2 cup shortening, unsweetened peanut butter or similar substitute for 1 stick .)

- Flour - 1 cup all purpose (Make this with Gluten Free flour)

- Salt 1/2 tsp

- Baking Powder- 1/2 tsp.

- Baking Soda- 1 tsp

- Unsweetened Ground Cinnamon-1 1/2 tsp

- Vanilla Extract- 1 tsp.

- Eggs- 2.

- Oats (Old Fashion or Quick (not instant))- 3 cups.

- Raisins- 1 1/4 cups.

How to make these cookies.

- Preheat your oven to 375. Prep a pan for nonstick - I use parchment paper.

- In a mixing bowl, creme together your sugar alternative and butter. Set this bowl aside.

- Now in another bowl, mix together the flour, salt, baking powder, baking soda, and cinnamon.

- Add the dry ingredients to the first bowl with the butter. Add the vanilla extract and eggs one at a time. Mix these gently (not fully).

- Stir in the oats and raisins until everything is blended.

- Bake this for 10-12 minutes or until the cookies begin to brown on the edges. Remove from oven and allow to site on the pan for a couple of minutes.

Thank you for purchasing this book about baking with sugar alternatives.

What did you think about this book?

Was this book helpful to you?

Is there anything that you think needs to be added in a book update or future release?

Please stop by the sugarfreediva.com and let me know what you think about this book, what topics you would like to see in the future (including recipes) or just to say hello

How to Measure Sugar Alternatives
1 cup of sugar=

Agave Nectar*- 2/3 cup
Coconut Palm Sugar- 1 cup
Erythritol- 1 1/3 cup
Equal- 25 packets or EQUAL SPOONFUL 1 cup
Honey*- substitute 1/2 to 2/3 cup honey.
Maple Syrup- 1/2 cup
Molasses- 1/2 cup

SPLENDA® NO CALORIE SWEETENER, GRANULATED- 1 cup
SPLENDA® No Calorie Sweetener and SPLENDA® Naturals Stevia Sweetener Packets- 24 packets
SPLENDA® Sugar Blend- 1/2 cup
SPLENDA® Brown Sugar Blend- 1 cup

Stevia- Equivalent Stevia powdered extract 1 teaspoon or Equivalent Stevia liquid concentrate 1 teaspoon

SweetLeaf®- 24 packets or 2 tbsp shaker or 4 tsp drops or 1/2 tsp extract powder or 2/3 cup Sugarleaf
Truvia Natural Sweetener- 1/3 cup+ 1 1/2 tbs or 24 packets.
Truvia Brown Sugar Blend- 1/2 cup
Truvia Baking Blend- 1/2 cup
Truvia Nectar- 1/4 cup+ 1 tbsp+ 2 tsp
Xylitol- 1 cup

SFD

TheSugarFreeDiva.com
see site for more details

Made in the USA
Monee, IL
06 February 2023

27247488R00043